1968 U.K. YEARBOOK

ISBN: 9781790423033

This book gives a fascinating and informative insight into life in the United Kingdom in 1968. It includes everything from the most popular music of the year to the cost of a buying a new house. Additionally there are chapters covering people in high office, the best-selling films of the year and all the main news and events. Want to know which team won the FA Cup or which British personalities were born in 1968? All this and much more awaits you within.

© Liberty Eagle Publishing Ltd. 2017
All Rights Reserved

INDEX

	Page
Calendar	4
People In High Office	5
News & Events	9
Births - UK Personalities	19
Popular Music	26
Top 5 Films	32
Sporting Winners	48
Cost Of Living	56

FIRST EDITION

1968

January
M	T	W	T	F	S	S
1	2	3	4	5	6	7
8	9	10	11	12	13	14
15	16	17	18	19	20	21
22	23	24	25	26	27	28
29	30	31				

◐:7 ○:15 ◑:22 ●:29

February
M	T	W	T	F	S	S
			1	2	3	4
5	6	7	8	9	10	11
12	13	14	15	16	17	18
19	20	21	22	23	24	25
26	27	28	29			

◐:6 ○:14 ◑:21 ●:28

March
M	T	W	T	F	S	S
				1	2	3
4	5	6	7	8	9	10
11	12	13	14	15	16	17
18	19	20	21	22	23	24
25	26	27	28	29	30	31

◐:7 ○:14 ◑:21 ●:28

April
M	T	W	T	F	S	S
1	2	3	4	5	6	7
8	9	10	11	12	13	14
15	16	17	18	19	20	21
22	23	24	25	26	27	28
29	30					

◐:6 ○:13 ◑:19 ●:27

May
M	T	W	T	F	S	S
		1	2	3	4	5
6	7	8	9	10	11	12
13	14	15	16	17	18	19
20	21	22	23	24	25	26
27	28	29	30	31		

◐:5 ○:12 ◑:19 ●:27

June
M	T	W	T	F	S	S
					1	2
3	4	5	6	7	8	9
10	11	12	13	14	15	16
17	18	19	20	21	22	23
24	25	26	27	28	29	30

◐:4 ○:10 ◑:17 ●:25

July
M	T	W	T	F	S	S
1	2	3	4	5	6	7
8	9	10	11	12	13	14
15	16	17	18	19	20	21
22	23	24	25	26	27	28
29	30	31				

◐:3 ○:10 ◑:17 ●:25

August
M	T	W	T	F	S	S
			1	2	3	4
5	6	7	8	9	10	11
12	13	14	15	16	17	18
19	20	21	22	23	24	25
26	27	28	29	30	31	

◐:1 ○:8 ◑:16 ●:24 ◐:31

September
M	T	W	T	F	S	S
						1
2	3	4	5	6	7	8
9	10	11	12	13	14	15
16	17	18	19	20	21	22
23	24	25	26	27	28	29
30						

○:6 ◑:14 ●:22 ◐:29

October
M	T	W	T	F	S	S
	1	2	3	4	5	6
7	8	9	10	11	12	13
14	15	16	17	18	19	20
21	22	23	24	25	26	27
28	29	30	31			

○:6 ◑:14 ●:21 ◐:28

November
M	T	W	T	F	S	S
				1	2	3
4	5	6	7	8	9	10
11	12	13	14	15	16	17
18	19	20	21	22	23	24
25	26	27	28	29	30	

○:5 ◑:13 ●:20 ◐:27

December
M	T	W	T	F	S	S
						1
2	3	4	5	6	7	8
9	10	11	12	13	14	15
16	17	18	19	20	21	22
23	24	25	26	27	28	29
30	31					

○:5 ◑:13 ●:19 ◐:26

PEOPLE IN HIGH OFFICE

Monarch - Queen Elizabeth II
Reign: 6th February 1952 - Present
Predecessor: King George VI
Heir Apparent: Charles, Prince Of Wales

United Kingdom

Prime Minister - Harold Wilson
Labour Party
16th October 1964 - 19th June 1970

New Zealand

Prime Minister
Keith Holyoake
12th December 1960 -
7th February 1972

Ireland

Taoiseach
Jack Lynch
10th November 1966 -
14th March 1973

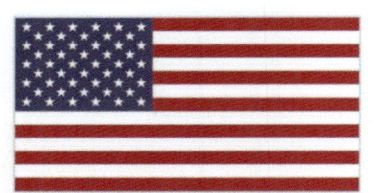

United States

President
Lyndon B. Johnson
22nd November 1963 -
20th January 1969

	Australia	Prime Ministers John McEwen (1967-1968) John Gorton (1968-1971)
	Brazil	President Artur da Costa e Silva (1967-1969)
	Canada	Prime Ministers Lester B. Pearson (1963-1968) Pierre Trudeau (1968-1979)
	China	Communist Party Leader Mao Zedong (1935-1976)
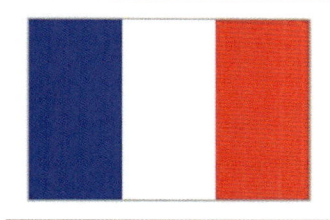	France	President Charles de Gaulle (1959-1969)
	India	Prime Minister Indira Gandhi (1966-1977)
	Israel	Prime Minister Levi Eshkol (1963-1969)
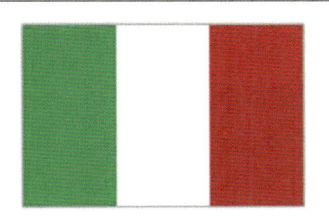	Italy	Prime Ministers Aldo Moro (1963-1968) Giovanni Leone (1968) Mariano Rumor (1968-1970)

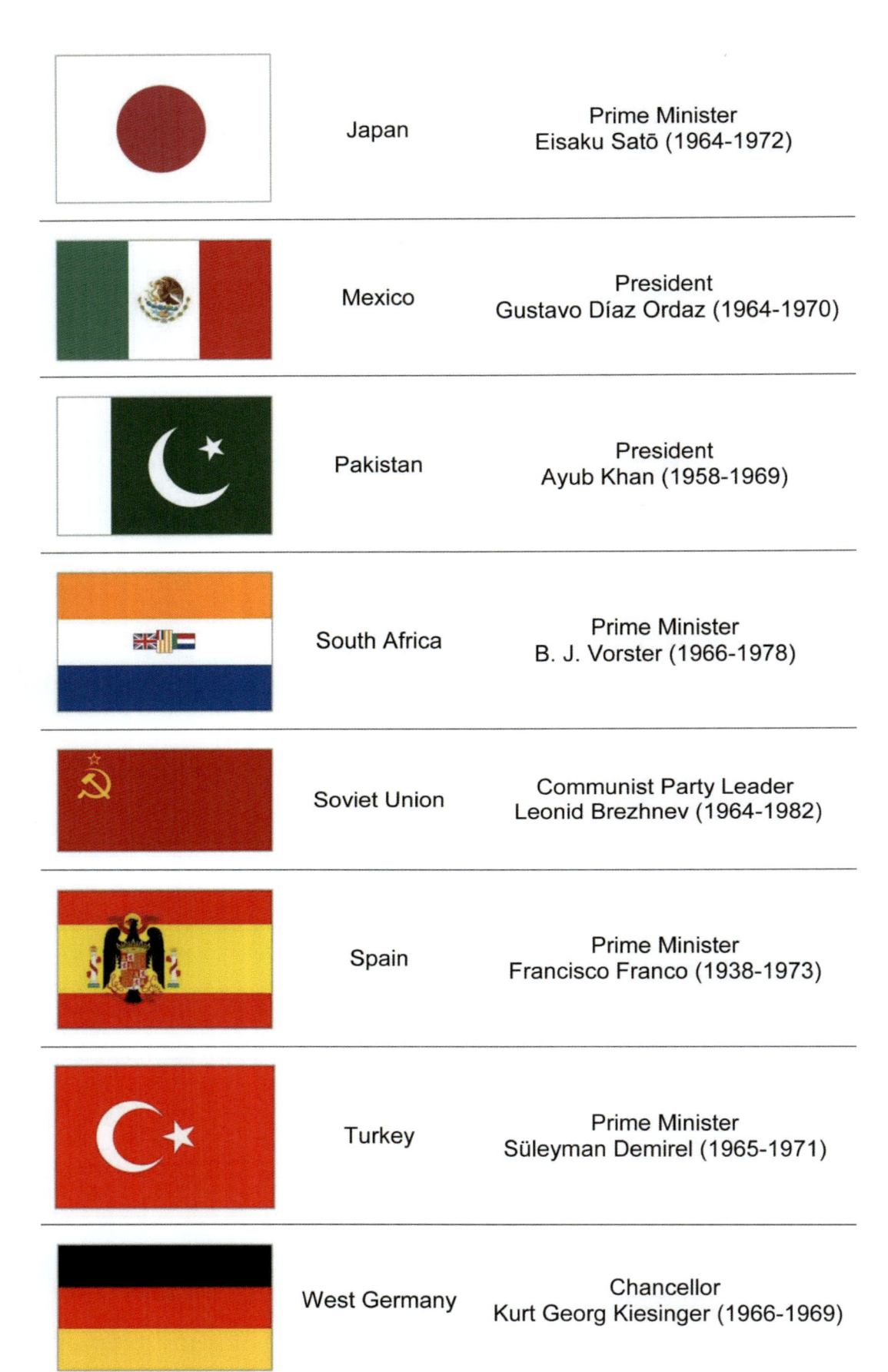

	Japan	Prime Minister Eisaku Satō (1964-1972)
	Mexico	President Gustavo Díaz Ordaz (1964-1970)
	Pakistan	President Ayub Khan (1958-1969)
	South Africa	Prime Minister B. J. Vorster (1966-1978)
	Soviet Union	Communist Party Leader Leonid Brezhnev (1964-1982)
	Spain	Prime Minister Francisco Franco (1938-1973)
	Turkey	Prime Minister Süleyman Demirel (1965-1971)
	West Germany	Chancellor Kurt Georg Kiesinger (1966-1969)

BRITISH NEWS & EVENTS

JAN

	The Ford Escort is introduced at Brussels Motor Show to replace the Anglia. Designed and manufactured by Ford UK a total of 1,594,486 Anglias were produced between 1939 and 1967.
1st	Cecil Day-Lewis is announced as the new Poet Laureate.
5th	Gardeners' World debuts on BBC1 and is presented by Ken Burras from Oxford Botanical Gardens. A year later Percy Thrower would take over as the main presenter.

8th January - Prime Minister Harold Wilson endorses the 'I'm Backing Britain' campaign encouraging workers to work extra time without pay or take other actions to help competitiveness. The campaign started spontaneously when five Surbiton secretaries volunteered to work an extra half-hour each day without pay to boost productivity and urged others to do the same. The invitation received an enormous response and a campaign took off spectacularly becoming a nationwide movement within a week.

16th	The Prime Minister announces that the Civil Defence Corps (CDC) is being stood down. The CDC was a civilian volunteer organisation established in Great Britain in 1949 to mobilise and take local control of an affected area in the aftermath of a major national emergency (principally envisaged as being a Cold War nuclear attack).

FEB

4th	96 Indians and Pakistanis arrive in Britain from Kenya where they are being forced out by increasingly draconian immigration laws. This brings the total number so far to 1,500.
6th - 18th	Great Britain and Northern Ireland compete at the Winter Olympics in Grenoble, France, but do not win any medals.

FEB

14th — Northampton is designated as a New Town with the Wilson government hoping to double its size and population by 1980.

24th — Jocelyn Bell Burnell, whilst studying and being advised by her thesis supervisor Antony Hewish at the University of Cambridge, announces the discovery of radio pulsars. Hewish later shared the Nobel Prize in Physics with astronomer Martin Ryle but controversially Bell Burnell was excluded despite having been the first to observe and precisely analyse the pulsars.

MAR

1st — The Commonwealth Immigrants Act of 1968 further reduces right of entry for citizens from the British Commonwealth to the U.K. It was introduced amid concerns that up to 200,000 Kenyan Asians fleeing that country's 'Africanisation' policy, would take up their right to reside in the UK. The bill went through parliament in three days, supported by the leadership of both the governing Labour and main opposition Conservative parties.

1st — Pupils of Colet Court preparatory school in Hammersmith stage the first performance of an Andrew Lloyd Webber-Tim Rice musical, Joseph and the Amazing Technicolor Dreamcoat.

2nd — Coal mining in the Black Country ends after some 300 years with the closure of Baggeridge Colliery near Sedgley.

12th — Mauritius achieves independence from British Rule. Sir Seewoosagur Ramgoolan becomes the independent nation's first Prime Minister, but Queen Elizabeth II still remains head of state.

15th — The Foreign Secretary George Brown resigns.

17th March - Protesters marched to the U.S. embassy in London's Grosvenor Square in a demonstration against U.S. involvement in the Vietnam War. More than 200 people were arrested after thousands of demonstrators clashed with mounted officers. The St John Ambulance Brigade stated that it had treated 86 people for injuries, 50 of which had to be taken to hospital, including 25 police officers.

APR

1st	Thames Valley Police is formed with the amalgamation of Berkshire Constabulary, Buckinghamshire Constabulary, Oxford City Police, Oxfordshire Constabulary and Reading Borough Police.
7th	Motor racing world champion Jim Clark, 32, is killed when his car leaves the track at 170mph and smashes into a tree during a Formula 2 race at Hockenheim.
11th	The popularity of Harold Wilson's Labour government is shown to be slumping as opinion polls show Edward Heath's Conservatives with a lead of more than 20 points.
18th	London Bridge is sold to American entrepreneur Robert P. McCulloch for £1,029,000. It is dismantled and rebuilt at Lake Havasu City, Arizona.
20th	Enoch Powell makes his controversial Rivers of Blood Speech on immigration.
21st	Enoch Powell is dismissed from the Shadow Cabinet by Opposition leader Edward Heath due to the Rivers of Blood Speech despite several opinion polls stating that the majority of the public shares Mr Powell's fears.
23rd	Five and ten pence coins are introduced in the run-up to Decimalisation. The full change over to the decimalised currency would occur on the 15th February 1971 (Decimal Day).
27th	The Abortion Act 1967 comes into effect. It legalises abortion on a number of grounds with free provision through the National Health Service.

MAY

3rd	Mr Frederick West (aged 45) becomes Britain's first heart transplant patient. A team of 18 doctors and nurses, led by South African-born surgeon Donald Ross, carry out the 7 hour operation at the National Heart Hospital in Marylebone, London. The donor was Patrick Ryan, 26, who died from a building site fall.
8th	The Kray Twins, 34-year-old Ronnie and Reggie, are among 18 men arrested in dawn raids across London. They stand accused of a series of crimes including murder, fraud, blackmail and assault. Their 41-year-old brother Charlie Kray is one of the other men under arrest.
11th	Manchester City FC win their second Football League First Division title.

14th May - Beatles John Lennon and Paul McCartney announce the creation of Apple Records at a New York press conference. The new company is to be owned equally between all 4 Beatles.

MAY

16th | Ronan Point, a 22-storey tower block in Newham, East London, collapses after a gas explosion killing four occupants. The explosion, only two months after the building had opened, blew out some load-bearing walls, causing the collapse of one entire corner of the building. The spectacular nature of the failure, caused by both poor design and poor construction, led to complete loss of public confidence in high-rise residential buildings and eventually led to major changes in UK building regulations.
18th | West Bromwich Albion beat Everton to win the FA Cup for the fifth time in front of 100,000 fans at Wembley Stadium. Jeff Astle scores the only goal in the third minute of extra time.
22nd | The General Assembly of the Church of Scotland permits the ordination of women as ministers.

29th May - Manchester United, watched by 92,225 fans at Wembley Stadium, become the first English winners of the European Cup after beating Benfica 4-1 in extra-time. The win marked the culmination of Manchester United's 10 years of rebuilding after the 1958 Munich air disaster, in which eight players had been killed and manager Matt Busby had been left fighting for his life. Captain Bobby Charlton and Bill Foulkes who had both survived the crash played in the game.

JUN

7th | Ford sewing machinists strike at the Dagenham assembly plant. The women workers are demanding pay comparable to that of men.
8th | Martin Luther King, Jr.'s killer, James Earl Ray, is arrested at London's Heathrow Airport while trying to leave the United Kingdom on a false Canadian passport. The UK quickly extradited Ray to Tennessee where he was charged with King's murder. He confessed to the crime on the 10th March 1969 (his 41st birthday) and after pleading guilty was sentenced to 99 years in prison.

JUN

10th	The National Health Service reintroduces prescription charges (now 2s 6d).
18th	Frederick West, Britain's first heart transplant patient, dies 46 days after his operation.
20th	Austin Currie, the Member of Parliament at Stormont in Northern Ireland, squats in a house in Caledon to protest discrimination in housing allocations.

JUL

	Cotton trading ceases at the Royal Exchange, Manchester.
4th	Alec Rose returns from a 354-day single-handed round-the-world sailing trip in his 36-foot cutter, Lively Lady. The voyage was closely followed by the British and international press and Rose's landfall at 12.33pm in Southsea was met by cheering crowds of hundreds of thousands. Six days later, on the 10th July 1968, he was made a Knight Bachelor.
10th	Torrential rain causes serious flooding in Bristol and across North East Somerset. Seven people lose their lives as towns and villages are inundated.
17th	The Beatles animated film Yellow Submarine debuts in London to widespread critical acclaim.
31st	The BBC sitcom Dad's Army, about the British Home Guard during the Second World War, is broadcast for the first time. It runs for 9 series (80 episodes) and regularly gains audiences of over 18 million viewers.

AUG

8th	The Royal Navy Leander-class frigate HMS Scylla is launched at Devonport, the last ship to be built at the Royal Dockyard.

11th August - British Rail runs its last steam train service and 4 steam locomotives make the 314-mile return passenger journey from Liverpool via Manchester to Carlisle. It was named the Fifteen Guinea Special because of the high cost of tickets (the equivalent of £250 today) but despite this 450 rail enthusiasts joined the tour to say their goodbyes to over 138 years of British history.

AUG

31st | The first Isle of Wight Festival takes place at Ford Farm near Godshill. 10,000 people turn up to watch acts including Jefferson Airplane. Arthur Brown, The Move, Smile, Tyrannosaurus Rex, Plastic Penny, Fairport Convention and The Pretty Things.

SEP

	The new school year in England sees the first local authorities adopt three tier education. Infant and junior schools are replaced by 5-8 or 5-9 first schools and 8-12 or 9-13 middle schools, with the transfer age to grammar and secondary modern schools being increased to 12 or 13.
	Japanese car maker Nissan began importing its range of Datsun badged family cars to Britain.
8th	British tennis player Virginia Wade defeats Billie Jean King to take the first U.S. Open Women's Singles title.
15th	The Great Flood of 1968, caused by a pronounced trough of low pressure, brings exceptionally heavy rain and thunderstorms to South East England.
16th	The General Post Office (officially established in England in 1660 by Charles II) divides post into first-class and second-class services.
26th	The Theatres Act 1968 ends censorship of the theatre.

27th September - The U.S. rock musical Hair opens in London following the removal of theatre censorship and runs for 1,997 performances. The musical's profanity, its depiction of the use of illegal drugs, its treatment of sexuality, its irreverence for the American flag, and its nude scene caused much comment and controversy.

OCT

2nd | The M1 motorway is completed when the final 35-mile section opens between Rotherham and Leeds.
Sheila Thorns from Birmingham gives birth to the first recorded instance of live Sextuplets in the UK on her 30th birthday. The babies, four boys and two girls, were delivered two months early but sadly three of them died in the weeks that followed.

OCT

5th	A civil rights march in Londonderry, Northern Ireland, which includes several Stormont and British MPs, turns violent after the Royal Ulster Constabulary tried to disperse the protesters by using batons and water cannon.
6th	British racing drivers Jackie Stewart, Graham Hill and John Surtees take the first three places at the United States Grand Prix.
8th	Enoch Powell warns that immigrants 'may change the character' of England.
12th - 27th	Great Britain and Northern Ireland compete at the Olympics in Mexico City and win 5 gold, 5 silver and 3 bronze medals.
14th	The rebuilt Euston railway station in London is opened by the Queen.
15th	Led Zeppelin make their first live performance at Surrey University.
18th	The National Girobank opens for business through the General Post Office. The organisation is widely credited for shaking up the UK banking market, forcing competitors to innovate and respond to the needs of the mass market.
27th	Police and protestors once again clash at an anti-Vietnam War protest outside the U.S. Embassy in London.
31st	Alan Bennett's play, Forty Years On, premiers at the Apollo Theatre in the West End. It is his first West End play.

NOV

18th	The James Watt Street fire: A warehouse fire in Glasgow kills 22 employees after they became trapped in a building behind barred windows, a hangover from its previous use as a whisky bond.
21st	The Cyril Lord carpet business goes into receivership.
22nd	The Kinks Are The Village Green Preservation Society, The Kinks sixth studio album, is released. The record is widely considered as one of their most influential and important works.
26th	The Race Relations Act is passed making it illegal to refuse housing, employment or public services to people in Britain because of their ethnic background.
29th	The Dawley New Town Amendment Order extends the boundaries of Dawley New Town in Shropshire and renames it Telford.
30th	The Trade Descriptions Act comes into force preventing shops and traders from describing goods in a misleading way.

DEC

	The official opening of first phase of the Royal Mint's new Llantrisant plant takes place in South Wales.
17th	Mary Flora Bell, an 11-year-old girl from Newcastle upon Tyne, is sentenced to life detention for the manslaughter of two small boys.

BRITISH PUBLICATIONS FIRST PRINTED IN 1968

- Agatha Christie's novel By The Pricking Of My Thumbs.
- Arthur C. Clarke's novel 2001: A Space Odyssey.
- Lawrence Durrell's novel Tunc (The Revolt Of Aphrodite - Book 1)
- Paul Scott's novel The Day Of The Scorpion (the second of the Raj Quartet).
- John Wyndham's novel Chocky.

NOTEABLE BRITISH DEATHS

27th Jan	Charles Henry Maxwell Knight, OBE (b. 9th July 1900). Spymaster, naturalist and broadcaster, reputedly a model for the James Bond character 'M'.
7th April	James 'Jim' Clark, Jr, OBE (b. 4th March 1936). Formula One racing driver who won the 1963 and 1965 World Championships.
7th May	Michael Henderson 'Mike' Spence (b. 30th December 1936). Racing driver who participated in 37 Formula One World Championship Grands Prix, achieving one podium and scoring a total of 27 championship points.
29th May	Major General Sir Stewart Graham Menzies, KCB, KCMG, DSO, MC (b. 30th January 1890). Chief of MI6 (Secret Intelligence Service) from 1939 to 1952.
21st Jun	William Earl Johns (b. 5th February 1893). Pilot and writer of adventure stories (usually written under the pen name Captain W. E. Johns) best remembered as the creator of the ace pilot and adventurer Biggles.

25th June - Anthony John 'Tony' Hancock (b. 12th May 1924). Comedian and actor who had huge success with his BBC series Hancock's Half Hour - Cast pictured above in rehearsals (left to right): Tony Hancock, Moira Lister, Bill Kerr and Sid James.

23rd Jul	Sir Henry Hallett Dale, OM, GBE, PRS (9th June 1875). Pharmacologist and physiologist who shared the 1936 Nobel Prize in Physiology or Medicine with Otto Loewi.
11th Sep	Thomas Dickson 'Tommy' Armour (24th September 1896). Professional golfer nicknamed The Silver Scot who was the winner of three major championships; the 1927 U.S. Open, 1930 PGA Championship and the 1931 Open Championship.
20th Oct	Bud Flanagan, OBE (14th October 1896). Popular music hall and vaudeville entertainer, comedian, television and film actor. He was best known as part of his double act with Chesney Allen.
28th Nov	Enid Mary Blyton (11th August 1897). Children's writer whose books have sold more than 600 million copies and have been translated into almost 90 languages. Blyton is best remembered today for her Noddy, Famous Five, Secret Seven, and Adventure series.

12 WORLDWIDE NEWS & EVENTS

1. 2nd January - Dr. Christiaan Barnard performs the third ever human heart transplant. South African dentist Philip Blaiberg survives for nineteen months before dying from heart complications but the success of the heart transplant led to an immediate increase in the number of doctors performing heart transplants around the world
2. 4th April - Martin Luther King Jr. is assassinated in Memphis, Tennessee. The Rev. Martin Luther King Jr. was standing on the second floor balcony of room 306 at the Lorraine Motel when he was struck by a bullet at 6:01pm. The 39-year-old civil rights leader was rushed to nearby St. Joseph's Hospital but never regained consciousness. He was pronounced dead at 7:05pm.
3. 5th June - U.S. presidential candidate Robert F. Kennedy is shot at the Ambassador Hotel in Los Angeles, California by Sirhan Sirhan. Kennedy, 42, dies from his injuries the following day.
4. 18th July - The semiconductor chip company Intel is founded by Gordon E. Moore and Robert Noyce in Mountain View, California.
5. September - The first Big Mac, costing 49 cents, was served in Pittsburgh, USA by a McDonald's franchise owner named Jim Delligatti.
6. 18th September - Soviet spacecraft Zond 5 becomes the first vehicle to circle the Moon and return to splashdown on Earth. It also carried the first Earthlings to reach the moon, including two tortoises, mealworms, wine flies, plants and other lifeforms, and was also the first to return moon travellers safely to Earth.

7. 30th September - Boeing introduces the first 747 'Jumbo Jet'. After its 1968 reveal the 747 made its first flight on the 9th February 1969 near Boeing's factory in western Washington state in the U.S. That specific plane flew more than 12,000 test flights but it never carried passengers for a major airline. The huge size of the aircraft was an aviation design milestone, more than six stories tall, it seated 374 passengers and weighed 300 tons.

8. 11th October - NASA launches the first manned Apollo mission, Apollo 7, with astronauts Wally Schirra, Donn Fulton Eisele and R. Walter Cunningham aboard. The goals for the mission included the first live television broadcast from orbit and testing the lunar module docking manoeuvre.

9. 22nd November - Star Trek airs American television's first interracial kiss. In the episode entitled Plato's Stepchildren, the crew aboard the Starship Enterprise become enslaved by humanoid Platonians who possess a telekinetic ability to force them to do anything the Platonians want them to do. Enterprise Capt. James Kirk, a white man played by William Shatner, is forced to kiss Nichelle Nichols' character, Lt. Nyota Uhura, a black woman. Censors at NBC insisted on filming an alternate version, sans smooch, fearing that local TV affiliates in the U.S. Deep South would refuse to air the episode. Shatner is reported to have purposefully ruined all the alternative takes so the network would be forced to air the kiss.

10. 3rd December - NBC television airs Elvis Presley's Comeback Special which becomes widely considered as one of the great moments in rock 'n' roll. The show was the highest-rated television special of the year and after its broadcast he began his stint in Las Vegas. He also toured and achieved a string of record-breaking sell-out performances across America. Chart successes returned including a U.S. No.1 in 1969 with Suspicious Minds and a U.K. No.1 with The Wonder Of You in 1970. Presley's informal jamming in front of a small audience in the special is regarded as a forerunner of the 'unplugged' concept, later popularised by MTV.

11. 9th December - In what becomes retrospectively known as 'The Mother of All Demos', Douglas Engelbart of Stanford Research Institute's Augmentation Research Center, demonstrates for the first time the computer mouse, the video conference, teleconferencing, hypertext, word processing, hypermedia, object addressing, the dynamic linker and a collaborative real-time editor using NLS.

12. 24th December - The First Manned Lunar Orbit: Apollo 8 enters the Moon's orbit and Frank Borman, Jim Lovell and William A. Anders become the first humans to see the far side of the Moon and planet Earth as a whole. At this time the first photographs of Earth from deep space by humans are taken including Anders now iconic photograph 'Earthrise'.

U.K. Personalities Born in 1968

Heather Anne Mills
12th January 1968

Media personality, model, businesswoman and activist. Mills first came to public attention in 1993 after a collision resulted in the amputation of her left leg below the knee. She continued to work as a model and sold her story to a tabloid newspaper. She received further public attention with her relationship and marriage to Sir Paul McCartney. After they divorced in 2008 Mills became involved in animal rights advocacy and is a patron of Viva! and the Vegetarian and Vegan Foundation. She is also vice-president of the Limbless Association.

Daniel Wroughton Craig
2nd March 1968

Actor who graduated from the Guildhall School of Music and Drama in 1991 before beginning his career on stage. His film debut was in the drama The Power Of One (1992). Other early appearances include the Disney film A Kid In King Arthur's Court (1995) and the biographical film Elizabeth (1998). Craig was cast as the fictional British secret agent James Bond in October 2005 for the film Casino Royale (2006). He has since played the character on 3 other occasions and is to star in Bond 25 which is expected to be released in November 2019.

Patricia Jude Francis Kensit
4th March 1968

British actress, singer, model and child star who first appeared on television in 1972 at the age of four in an advert for Birds Eye frozen peas. Kensit was lead singer of the band Eighth Wonder (1983-1989), played the role of Sadie King in the ITV soap opera Emmerdale (2004-2006) and played Faye Byrne in the BBC One medical drama Holby City (2007-2010). She has been married to musicians Dan Donovan, Jim Kerr, Liam Gallagher and Jeremy Healy.

Paul Charles Merson
20th March 1968

Former professional footballer and manager, turned football television pundit. Merson made his debut for Arsenal in the 1986-87 season and went on to play eleven seasons with the Gunners. He was a key player in the club's success winning the Football League Championship twice, the FA Cup, the Football League Cup and the European Cup Winners' Cup. He later played at a number of other clubs and made his final appearance in 2012 at the age of 43. During his football career Merson was also capped 21 times for England.

Michael Andrew Atherton, OBE
23rd March 1968

Broadcaster, journalist and former right-handed opening batsman for Lancashire and England. Atherton achieved the captaincy of England at the age of 25 and led the side in a record 54 Test matches. Following retirement he became a journalist and is currently a cricket commentator with Sky Sports and cricket correspondent for The Times. In 2002 he produced his autobiography: Opening Up and in 2006 published his book Gambling: A Story Of Triumph And Disaster.

Damon Albarn, OBE
23rd March 1968

Singer, songwriter and multi-instrumentalist. He is the lead singer of the rock band Blur and co-founder, vocalist, instrumentalist and principal songwriter of the virtual band Gorillaz. In 2008 The Daily Telegraph ranked Albarn number 18 in their list of the '100 most powerful people in British culture' and in a 2010 UK poll for Q magazine he was voted the fourth-greatest frontman of all time. Albarn was appointed Officer of the Order of the British Empire (OBE) in the 2016 New Year Honours for his services to music.

Nasser Hussain, OBE
28th March 1968

Former cricketer who captained the England cricket team between 1999 and 2003. Hussain scored over 30,000 runs from more than 650 matches across all first-class and List-A cricket, including 62 centuries. During his international career (1990-2004) he played in a total of 96 Test matches and 88 One Day International games. His 2005 autobiography, Playing With Fire, won the Best Autobiography category of the 2005 British Sports Book Awards.

Richard 'Ricky' Groves
23rd April 1968

Actor who trained at The Poor School in London and is best known for playing Garry Hobbs in EastEnders (2000-2009). In 2009 he took part in the seventh series of Strictly Come Dancing where he was paired with professional dancer Erin Boag (they were voted out in week 10). Other television appearances include All Star Family Fortunes, The Weakest Link Eastenders Special (2010), Celebrity Coach Trip with friend Alex Ferns (2010), Celebrity MasterChef (2011), Splash (2014) and Who's Doing the Dishes? (2016).

Howard Paul Donald
28th April 1968

English singer, songwriter, drummer, pianist, dancer, DJ and record producer. Donald is a member of pop-group Take That and as such has had 28 top 40 singles of which 12 have reached the No.1 spot. Take That have also had seven No.1 albums and received 8 Brit Awards (winning awards for Best British Group and Best British Live Act). They have also had massive international success with 56 No.1 singles and 37 No.1 albums around the world.

Ruth Maria Kelly
9th May 1968

Former Labour Party politician who served as the MP for Bolton West from 1997 until 2010. During her time in government Kelly served in a number of roles including the Secretary of State for Transport, Secretary of State for Communities and Local Government, Minister for Women and Equality and Secretary of State for Education and Skills. From May 2010 Kelly was the Global Head of Client Strategy at HSBC before leaving in 2015 to become Pro-Vice Chancellor for Research and Enterprise at St Mary's University, Twickenham.

Alastair James Hay 'Al' Murray
10th May 1968

Comedian and TV personality well known for his stand-up persona and quick repartee. Murray started out touring with fellow comedians including Harry Hill and Frank Skinner, and won the Perrier Award at the Edinburgh Festival Fringe in 1999. His best-known character is 'The Pub Landlord', a xenophobic publican. In 2003 Murray was listed in The Observer as one of the 50 funniest acts in British comedy and in 2007 he was voted the 16th greatest stand-up comic on Channel 4's 100 Greatest Stand-Ups.

Catherine Tate
12th May 1968

Comedian, actress, writer and winner of numerous awards for her work on the comedy sketch series The Catherine Tate Show. Following her success she went on to play Donna Noble in the 2006 Christmas special of Doctor Who and later reprised her role to become the Tenth Doctor's companion for the fourth series in 2008. In 2011 she began a recurring role as Nellie Bertram in the U.S. version of The Office and was a regular until the series ended in 2013.

Rebekah Mary Brooks
27th May 1968

Journalist and former newspaper editor who was chief executive officer of News International (2009-2011) having previously served as the youngest editor of a British national newspaper at News of the World (2000-2003) and the first female editor of The Sun (2003-2009). In September 2015 Brooks was confirmed as CEO of News UK, the renamed News International, re-establishing the working relationship with News Corp founder and chairman Rupert Murdoch.

Jonathan Peter 'Jon' Culshaw
2nd June 1968

Impressionist and comedian best known for his work on the radio and television comedy series Dead Ringers since 2000. Culshaw has also voiced a number of characters for ITV shows including 2DTV (2001), Spitting Image (1994-1996), Newzoids (2015-present), as well as appearing in The Impressions Show alongside Debra Stephenson since 2009. Some of his most famous impressions include Tony Blair, Obi-Wan Kenobi, Russell Crowe, George W. Bush, Ozzy Osbourne, Boris Johnson and Michael McIntyre.

Adam Brinley Woodyatt
28th June 1968

Actor best known for his role as Ian Beale in the long-running BBC soap opera EastEnders. He is the show's longest-serving actor and the only one to have appeared continuously since its inception in February 1985. Alongside Letitia Dean and Gillian Taylforth, who play Sharon Watts and Kathy Beale respectively, Woodyatt is one of only three members of the original cast currently in EastEnders. He is a recipient of 5 British Soap Awards including one for Best Actor as well as a recipient of a TRIC Award.

Olivia Haigh Williams
26th July 1968

Film, stage and television actress. After studying drama at the Bristol Old Vic Theatre School and Royal Shakespeare Company, her first significant role was as Jane Fairfax in the television film Emma (1996). She made her film debut in The Postman (1997), followed by Rushmore (1998) and The Sixth Sense (1999). Williams then appeared in several British films, including Lucky Break (2001), The Heart of Me (2002) and An Education (2009). In 2010 she won acclaim for her performance in Roman Polanski's The Ghost Writer.

Colin Steele McRae, MBE
5th August 1968 -
15th September 2007

Rally driver born in Lanark, Scotland who was the son of five-time British Rally Champion Jimmy McRae and brother of rally driver Alister McRae. Colin McRae was the 1991 and 1992 British Rally Champion and, in 1995, became the first British person and the youngest to win the World Rally Championship Drivers' title, a record he still holds. In November 2008 he was posthumously inducted into the Scottish Sports Hall of Fame.

Darren Christopher Clarke, OBE
14th August 1968

Professional golfer from Northern Ireland who currently plays on the European Tour and has previously played on the PGA Tour. He has won 21 tournaments worldwide on a number of golf's main tours including the European Tour, the PGA Tour, the Sunshine Tour and the Japan Golf Tour. His biggest victory came when he won the 2011 Open Championship at Royal St George's in England, his first major win after more than 20 years and 54 attempts.

Helen Elizabeth McCrory, OBE
17th August 1968

Actress who portrayed Cherie Blair in both The Queen (2006) and The Special Relationship (2010). She also portrayed Narcissa Malfoy in the final three Harry Potter films, Mama Jeanne in Martin Scorsese's family film Hugo (2011), Clair Dowar in the James Bond film Skyfall (2012), Polly Gray in Peaky Blinders (2013-present) and Emma Banville in Fearless (2017). McCrory was appointed an Officer of the Order of the British Empire (OBE) in the 2017 New Year Honours for services to drama.

Christopher Miles Boardman, MBE
26th August 1968

Former racing cyclist who won an individual pursuit gold medal at the 1992 Summer Olympics, broke the world hour record three times, and won three stages and wore the yellow jersey on three separate occasions at the Tour de France. In 1992 he was awarded an MBE for services to cycling. Boardman is now involved in producing commercial and competition bikes with the companies Boardman Bikes and Boardman Elite ventures.

Julia Sawalha
9th September 1968

Actress known mainly for her role as Saffron Monsoon in the BBC sitcom Absolutely Fabulous. She is also known for portraying Lynda Day, editor of the Junior Gazette, in Press Gang and Lydia Bennet in the 1995 television miniseries of Jane Austen's Pride And Prejudice. Additionally she has played Dorcas Lane in the BBC's costume drama Lark Rise To Candleford, Carla Borrego in Jonathan Creek and Jan Ward on the 2014 BBC One mystery Remember Me.

Naomi Ellen Watts
28th September 1968

Actress and film producer who made her screen debut in the Australian drama film For Love Alone (1986). She first came to attention though in David Lynch's psychological thriller Mulholland Drive (2001) and a year later enjoyed box-office success as Rachel Keller in The Ring (2002). Since then Watts's success has continued with films such as 21 Grams (2003), King Kong (2005), Fair Game (2010), J. Edgar (2011) and The Impossible (2012).

Matthew 'Matt' Weston Goss (left)
Luke Damon Goss (right)
29th September 1968

Twin brothers Matt (lead singer) and Luke Goss (drummer) who, along with Craig Logan (bass player), formed Bros in 1986. The band was managed by former Pet Shop Boys manager Tom Watkins and achieved chart success, and a large teenage fanbase, in 1988 with songs such as When Will I Be Famous and I Owe You Nothing. Logan quit the band in 1989 and the Goss twins continued as a duo. In 1992, after two more albums with less success, the band split up. Bros reformed for a number of UK shows in 2017.

Victoria Antoinette Derbyshire
2nd October 1968

BAFTA award-winning journalist and broadcaster whose current affairs and debate programme has been broadcast on BBC Two and the BBC News Channel since 2015. She has formerly presented Newsnight, Watchdog and the morning news, current affairs and interview programme on BBC Radio 5 Live. At the 2011 Sony Awards she won the Gold Award for Best News & Current Affairs Programme and, in 2012 and 2014, the Speech Broadcaster Of The Year Award.

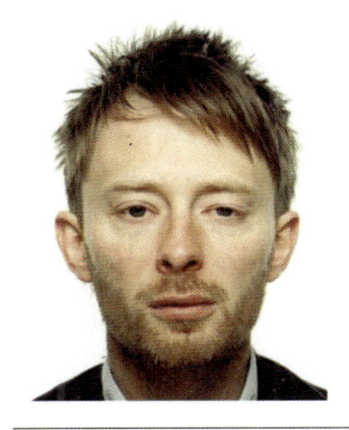

Thomas Edward 'Thom' Yorke
7th October 1968

Musician and composer best known as the singer and principal songwriter of the alternative rock band Radiohead. A multi-instrumentalist Yorke is known for his falsetto vocals and in 2008 Rolling Stone ranked him the 66th greatest singer of all time. To date Radiohead have sold more than 30 million albums worldwide, won 4 Grammy Awards, 4 Ivor Novello Awards, 9 NME Awards and received the Best Act In The World Today award three times at the Q Awards.

Matthew Le Tissier
14th October 1968

Former professional footballer and honorary president of Guernsey F.C. who works as a football pundit for Sky Sports. Le Tissier spent his entire professional club career with Southampton and won eight caps for the England national football team. Le Tissier is the second-highest ever scorer for Southampton and was voted PFA Young Player of the Year in 1990. He was the first midfielder to score 100 goals in the Premier League and is notable for his record at penalty kicks, scoring from the spot 47 times from 48 attempts.

Katherine 'Kate' Humble
12th December 1968

Television presenter of wildlife and science programmes. Humble started her television career as a researcher, later transferring to presenting programmes such as Top Gear, Tomorrow's World and the 2001 series Holiday - You Call The Shots. She has specialised in presenting wildlife programmes including Animal Park, Springwatch, Autumnwatch, Wild In Africa and Seawatch. and served as President of the RSPB from 2009 until 2013.

1968 TOP 10 SINGLES

No.1	Louis Armstrong	What A Wonderful World / Cabaret
No.2	Mary Hopkin	Those Were The Days
No.3	Des O'Connor	I Pretend
No.4	Hugo Montenegro	The Good, The Bad And The Ugly
No.5	The Union Gap Featuring Gary Puckett	Young Girl
No.6	Tommy James & The Shondells	Mony Mony
No.7	The Beatles	Hey Jude
No.8	The Equals	Baby Come Back
No.9	Esther & Abi Ofarim	Cinderella Rockefella
No.10	Tom Jones	Delilah

① Louis Armstrong
What A Wonderful World

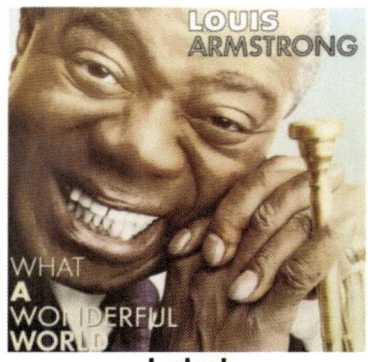

Label:
EMI Electrola

Written by:
G. D. Weiss / G. Douglas

Length:
2 mins 15 secs

Louis Daniel Armstrong (b. 4th August 1901- d. 6th July 1971), nicknamed Satchmo, Satch or Pops, was an American trumpeter, composer, singer and occasional actor who was one of the most influential figures in jazz. His career spanned five decades, from the 1920s to the 1960s, and different eras in the history of jazz. Armstrong was posthumously awarded the Grammy Lifetime Achievement Award in 1972 by the Academy of Recording Arts and Sciences. He has also had 12 recordings inducted into the Grammy Hall Of Fame including 'What A Wonderful World'.

---

② Mary Hopkin
Those Were The Days

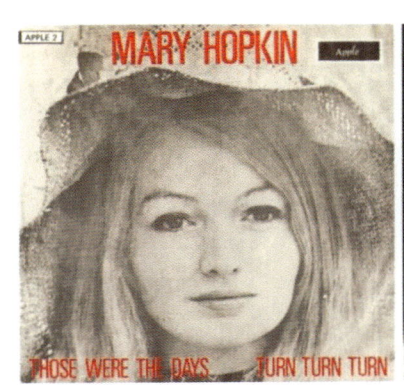

Label:
Apple Records

Written by:
Gene Raskin

Length:
5 mins 11 secs

Mary Hopkin (b. 3rd May 1950), credited on some recordings as Mary Visconti, is a Welsh folk singer and one of the first musicians to sign to The Beatles' Apple label. She is best known for her debut No.1 single 'Those Were The Days' which was produced by Paul McCartney and released on the 30th August 1968. The record was a phenomenal success with global sales of over 8,000,000.

3. Des O'Connor — I Pretend

Label: Columbia
Written by: Barry Mason / Les Reed
Length: 2 mins 49 secs

Desmond Bernard 'Des' O'Connor, CBE (b. 12th January 1932) is a comedian, broadcaster and singer. O'Connor has recorded 36 albums and has had four top-ten singles throughout his career, with global sales of over 10 million records. His only No.1 recording came with 'I Pretend' which climbed to the top of the UK and Ireland singles charts in July 1968. In 2001 he was presented with the Special Recognition Award at the National Television Awards for his contributions to television and in 2008 was appointed a Commander of the Order of the British Empire (CBE).

4. Hugo Montenegro — The Good, The Bad And The Ugly

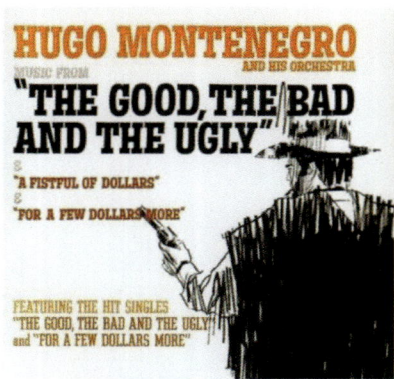

Label: RCA
Written by: Ennio Morricone
Length: 2 mins 43 secs

Hugo Mario Montenegro (b. 2nd September 1925 - d. 6th February 1981) was an orchestra leader and composer of film soundtracks. His best known work is derived from interpretations of the music from Spaghetti Westerns, especially his cover version of Ennio Morricone's main theme from the 1966 film The Good, The Bad And The Ugly.

5. The Union Gap Featuring Gary Puckett
Young Girl

Label:
CBS

Written by:
Jerry Fuller

Length:
3 mins 12 secs

Gary Puckett & the Union Gap (initially credited as The Union Gap featuring Gary Puckett) were an American pop rock group active in the late 1960s. Their biggest hits in the UK were Young Girl, their only No.1, and Lady Willpower, which made it to No.5 in the charts. The group was formed in 1967 by Gary Puckett, Gary 'Mutha' Withem, Dwight Bement, Kerry Chater and Paul Wheatbread.

---

6. Tommy James & The Shondells
Mony Mony

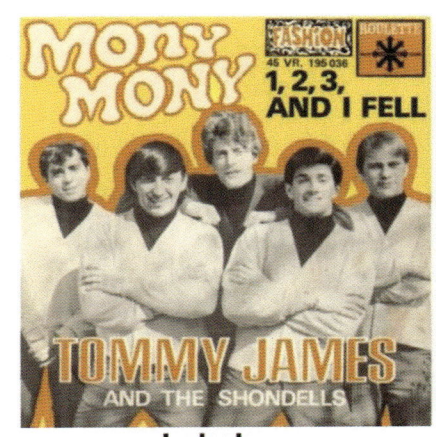

Label:
Roulette

Written by:
B. Bloom / T. James

Length:
2 mins 45 secs

Tommy James and the Shondells are an American rock band formed in Niles, Michigan in 1960. Mony Mony was their only UK hit record reaching the No.1 spot in August 1968. They did have more success though in their home country with two No.1 singles and twelve other Top 40 hits including five in the Billboard Hot 100 top ten.

The Beatles
Hey Jude

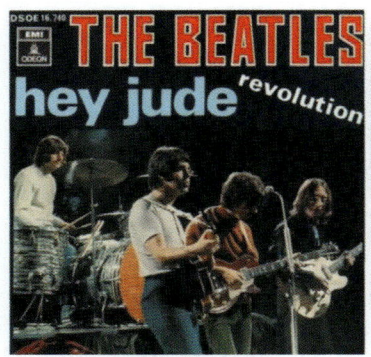

Label:
Apple Records

Written by:
John Lennon / Paul McCartney

Length:
7 mins 11 secs

The Beatles were a rock band formed in Liverpool in 1960. With members John Lennon, Paul McCartney, George Harrison and Ringo Starr they became widely regarded as the greatest and most influential act of the rock era. They have had more No.1 albums on the British charts and sold more singles in the UK than any other act. They have received ten Grammy Awards, an Academy Award for Best Original Song Score and fifteen Ivor Novello Awards. Collectively, included in Time magazine's compilation of the twentieth century's 100 most influential people, they are the best-selling band in history with estimated sales of over 600 million records worldwide.

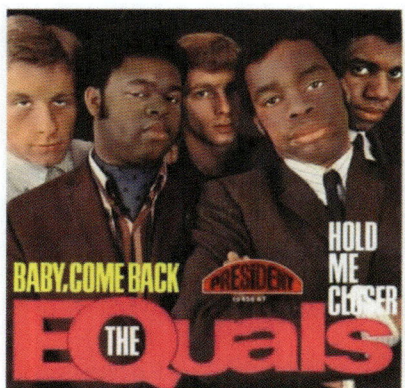

The Equals
Baby Come Back

Label:
President Records

Written by:
Eddy Grant

Length:
2 mins 35 secs

The Equals were a British pop, R&B and rock group formed in North London in 1965. They are mainly remembered for their million-selling chart-topper 'Baby, Come Back'. Eddy Grant founded the group with John Hall, Pat Lloyd and twin brothers Derv and Lincoln Gordon.

Esther & Abi Ofarim
Cinderella Rockefella

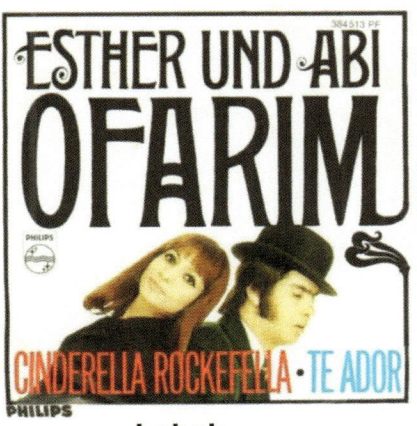

Label:
Philips

Written by:
Mason Williams / Nancy Ames

Length:
2 mins 29 secs

Esther & Abi Ofarim were a married Israeli musical duo who in 1966 had their first hit in Germany with 'Noch Einen Tanz'. Their greatest success in Germany came the next year with 'Morning Of My Life', written by the Bee Gees. In 1968 'Cinderella Rockefella' hit the top of the charts in a number of countries including the UK. After the couple divorced the duo broke up and Esther undertook a successful solo career.

Tom Jones
Delilah

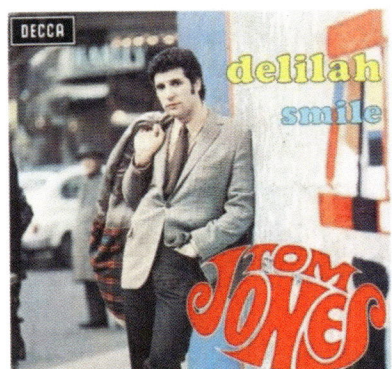

Label:
Decca

Written by:
Barry Mason / Les Reed

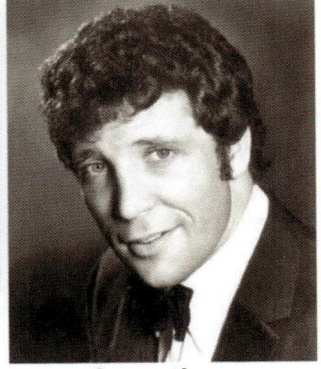

Length:
3 mins 20 secs

Sir Thomas Jones Woodward, OBE (b. 7th June 1940) is a Welsh singer known by his stage name Tom Jones. He became one of the most popular vocalists to emerge from the mid-1960s and has sung nearly every form of popular music including pop, rock, R&B, show tunes, country, dance, soul and gospel. Jones has sold over 100 million records and had 36 Top 40 hits in the UK.

1968: TOP FILMS

1. **2001: A Space Odyssey** - *Metro-Goldwyn-Mayer*
2. **Funny Girl** - *Columbia Pictures*
3. **The Love Bug** - *Walt Disney Productions*
4. **The Odd Couple** - *Paramount Pictures*
5. **Bullitt** - *Warner Bros. / Seven Arts*

OSCARS

Best Picture: Oliver!

Best Director: Carol Reed (Oliver!)

Best Actor:
Cliff Robertson (*Charly*)

Best Actress (Shared):
Katharine Hepburn (*The Lion in Winter*)
Barbra Streisand (*Funny Girl*)

Best Supporting Actor:
Jack Albertson (*The Subject Was Roses*)

Best Supporting Actress:
Ruth Gordon (*Rosemary's Baby*)

2001: A SPACE ODYSSEY

Directed by: Stanley Kubrick - Runtime: 149 minutes

A large black monolith is found beneath the surface of the moon and the point of origin is confirmed as Jupiter. An expedition is sent out with the hopes of finding the source but events take a turn as Dr. David Bowman discovers faults in the spacecraft's communications system HAL.

STARRING

Keir Dullea
Born: 30th May 1936

Character:
Dr. David Bowman

Actor of television, stage and film who made his movie debut as juvenile delinquent Billy Lee Jackson in Hoodlum Priest (1961). Dullea has had a long and successful career on the stage but is best known for his portrayal of astronaut Dave Bowman in 2001: A Space Odyssey and in 2010: The Year We Make Contact (1984). Other film roles include Bunny Lake Is Missing (1965) and Black Christmas (1974).

Gary Lockwood
Born: 21st February 1937

Character:
Dr. Frank Poole

Actor (born John Gary Yurosek) who is primarily known for his roles as astronaut Frank Poole in 2001: A Space Odyssey and as Lieutenant Commander Gary Mitchell in the Star Trek pilot episode 'Where No Man Has Gone Before' (1966). Lockwood had a regular supporting role in Follow The Sun (1961-1962), the title role of The Lieutenant (1963-1964), and from the early 1960s into the mid-1990s played numerous guest television roles.

William Sylvester
Born: 31st January 1922
Died: 25th January 1995

Character:
Dr. Heywood R. Floyd

Television and film actor whose most famous film credit was as Dr. Heywood Floyd in Stanley Kubrick's 2001: A Space Odyssey. Sylvester served in the U.S. Navy during the Second World War and settled in Britain after the war to pursue his interest in professional acting. Among his many television credits were; a 1959 BBC version of Shakespeare's Julius Caesar (playing Mark Antony), The Saint, The High Chaparral, Harry O, The Six Million Dollar Man and Quincy, M.E.

TRIVIA

Goofs | As astronaut Dave Bowman climbs into HAL's logic centre the seal on his suit's left hand is broken and the glove separates from the suit. The glove is reattached once he enters the logic centre.

The Moon changes phase several times (backwards and forwards) in the long shots during the trip from the Space Station to Clavius Base on the Moon.

Interesting Facts | The main Discovery set was built by aircraft manufacturer Vickers-Armstrong inside a 12m x 2m drum designed to rotate at 3mph. It cost $750,000.

CONTINUED

Interesting Facts In the premier screening of the film 241 people walked out of the theatre including Rock Hudson, who said, "Will someone tell me what the hell this is about?" Arthur C. Clarke once said, "If you understand '2001' completely, we failed. We wanted to raise far more questions than we answered."

There is no dialogue in the first 25 or in last 23 minutes of the movie. In total there are around 88 dialogue-free minutes in the film.

Stanley Kubrick worked for several months with effects technicians to come up with a convincing effect for the floating pen in the shuttle sequence. After trying many different techniques, without success, Kubrick decided to simply use a pen that was adhered (using newly invented double-sided tape) to a sheet of glass and suspended in front of the camera. In fact, the shuttle attendant can be seen to 'pull' the pen off the glass when she takes hold of it.

The actual 'Space Station 5' model, which was about seven feet across, was found discarded in a field a few years after this film was made. Unfortunately the model was then destroyed by vandals a few days later.

The only Oscar won by the film was for special visual effects. It was awarded to Stanley Kubrick and was his sole win from 13 nominations. However, while Kubrick designed much of the look of the film and its effects, many of the technicians involved felt it was wrong for him to receive the sole credit. The Academy tightened its eligibility rules following this controversy.

Quotes **HAL:** I know I've made some very poor decisions recently but I can give you my complete assurance that my work will be back to normal. I've still got the greatest enthusiasm and confidence in the mission. And I want to help you.

(On Dave's return to the ship after HAL has killed the rest of the crew)
HAL: Look Dave, I can see you're really upset about this. I honestly think you ought to sit down calmly, take a stress pill, and think things over.

FUNNY GIRL

Directed by: William Wyler - Runtime: 151 minutes

The vibrant and beautiful young Fanny Brice starts out as a bit player on the New York City vaudeville stage but works her way up to stardom on Broadway. Valued for her vocal and comedic talents by theatre impresario Florenz Ziegfeld Jr., Fanny thrives, but her relationship with her suave businessman husband, Nick Arnstein, is another story.

STARRING

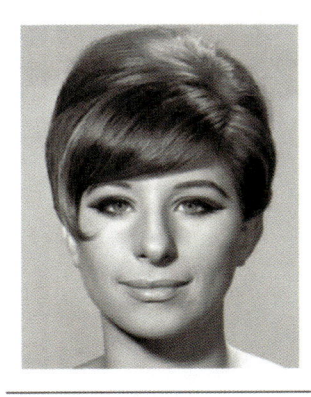

Barbra Streisand
Born: 24th April 1942

Character:
Fanny Brice

Singer, songwriter, actress and filmmaker. During a career spanning six decades she has become an icon in multiple fields of entertainment winning two Academy Awards (for Funny Girl and the 1976 film A Star Is Born), ten Grammys, five Emmys, a Special Tony Award, an American Film Institute Award, a Kennedy Center Honors prize, four Peabody Awards and nine Golden Globes. In 2015 she was awarded the Presidential Medal of Freedom by Barack Obama.

Omar Sharif
Born: 10th April 1932
Died: 10th July 2015

Character:
Nick Arnstein

Egyptian actor who began his career in his native country in the 1950s but is best known for his appearances in both British and American productions. Some of his most notable films include Lawrence Of Arabia (1962), Doctor Zhivago (1965) and Funny Girl. Sharif spoke Arabic, English, Greek, French, Spanish, Portuguese and Italian fluently, and at one time ranked among the world's top contract bridge players.

Kay Medford
Born: 14th September 1919
Died: 10th April 1980

Character:
Rose Brice

Character actress and comedian who made her Broadway debut in 1951 in the musical Paint Your Wagon. Later she appeared onstage in Funny Girl, for which she was nominated for the 1964 Tony Award for a Featured Actress in a Musical. When she repeated the role in the 1968 film adaptation she was nominated for an Academy Award for Best Supporting Actress. Medford had numerous other film and television credits throughout her 38 year career.

TRIVIA

Goofs | When Nick leaves after meeting Fanny for the first time, Fanny walks toward a blue door with a window. The door then turns solid and the window disappears.

When in Baltimore, Fanny and Nick come out of a restaurant and lean on a post. In the next scene they are further down the pier and leaning on a different post.

Interesting Facts | Funny Girl was originally a musical on Broadway and was based on the real-life story of Fanny Brice. It ran for 1348 performances between 1964 and 1967.

CONTINUED

Interesting Facts

Barbra Streisand was, at the time of the film's release, a voting member of AMPAS. When she found out she had been nominated, she, like any member nominated, voted for herself. If she hadn't she wouldn't have tied with Katharine Hepburn for the year's Best Actress Oscar.

Several co-stars publicly blasted Barbra Streisand and director William Wyler for much of their scenes being cut in favour of focusing almost entirely on Streisand.

Barbra Streisand and Omar Sharif had an affair that lasted for the duration of the production. This would contribute to the end of her marriage to Elliott Gould. William Wyler, who knew about the affair, tried to channel their real-life chemistry into their performances.

Frank Sinatra was seriously considered for the role of Nicky Arnstein but Barbra Streisand vetoed his casting because, while she respected his talent, she disliked him personally.

William Wyler was asked by a friend whether Barbra Streisand had been hard to work with. He replied, "No, not too hard, considering it was the first movie she ever directed."

Quotes

(First line - looking in the mirror)
Fanny Brice: Hello, gorgeous.

Fanny Brice: Where I come from, when two people... well, sort of love each other... oh, never mind.
Nick Arnstein: Well? What do they do when they "sort of love each other"?
Fanny Brice: Well, one of them says, "Why don't we get married?"
Nick Arnstein: Really?
Fanny Brice: Yeah, and sometimes it's even the man.

THE LOVE BUG

Directed by: Robert Stevenson - Runtime: 108 minutes

Down-on-his-luck race car driver Jim Douglas teams up with Herbie, a Volkswagen Beetle with a mind of its own, from showroom to the race track, and various close escapes in between.

STARRING

Dean Carroll Jones
Born: 25th January 1931
Died: 1st September 2015

Character:
Jim Douglas

Actor who started his film career by signing a contract at MGM, beginning with a small role as a soldier in Somebody Up There Likes Me (1956) and then playing disc jockey Teddy Talbot in the Elvis Presley film Jailhouse Rock (1957). Jones is best known for his roles as Agent Zeke Kelso in That Darn Cat! (1965), Jim Douglas in The Love Bug, Albert Dooley in The Million Dollar Duck (1971) and Dr. Herman Varnick in Beethoven (1992).

Michele Lee
Born: 24th June 1942

Character:
Carole Bennett

Actress, singer, dancer, producer and director, who began her career on Broadway in Vintage 60 (1960). She is best known for her role as Karen Cooper Fairgate MacKenzie on the prime-time soap opera Knots Landing (1979-1993), for which she was nominated for a 1982 Emmy Award and won the Soap Opera Digest Award for Best Actress in 1988, 1991 and 1992. She was the only performer to appear in all 344 episodes of the series.

David Cecil MacAlister Tomlinson
Born: 7th May 1917
Died: 24th June 2000

Character:
Peter Thorndyke

Actor on stage, film and television, and a comedian. Having been described as both a leading man and a character actor, he is primarily remembered for his roles as authority figure George Banks in Mary Poppins (1964), magician Professor Emelius Browne in Bedknobs and Broomsticks (1971) and as hapless antagonist Peter Thorndyke in The Love Bug. In 2002, two years after his death, Tomlinson was posthumously inducted as a Disney Legend.

TRIVIA

Goofs | When Tennessee is hanging out of Herbie over a cliff, the number 53 is missing from Herbie's passenger door.

When Jim climbs out from the overturned car in the opening sequence his helmet's chinstrap can be seen loosely dangling. He then dramatically removes the chinstrap to throw off his helmet.

Interesting Facts | The movie was made and released seven years after its source novel Car, Boy, Girl (1961) by Gordon Buford was first published.

CONTINUED

Interesting Facts Dean Jones personally requested to play the hippy at the drive-in restaurant. The director originally turned him down but after Jones proved that he could convincingly take on the persona he was immediately given the part.

The station attendant at Tang Wu's Quick Service is wearing a jacket bearing the phrase 'Put a Dragon in Your Tank'. This is a reference to the 1960s advertising slogan 'Put a Tiger in Your Tank' used by the Esso oil corporation.

Quotes **Carole:** Help! I'm a prisoner! I can't get out!
Van Hippy: We all prisoners, chickee-baby. We all locked in.
(Van Hippy looks over at his hippy partner as Carole bangs on the window)
Van Hippy: Huh, a couple of weirdos, Guenivere.

Jim Douglas: I may be kidding myself but I think I can make something out of that sad little bucket of bolts.

THE ODD COUPLE

PARAMOUNT PICTURES presents

Jack Lemmon and **Walter Matthau** are **The Odd Couple**

...say no more.

Directed by: Gene Saks - Runtime: 105 minutes

Two friends try sharing an apartment but their ideas of housekeeping and lifestyles are as different as night and day.

STARRING

Jack Lemmon
Born: 8th February 1925
Died: 27th June 2001

Character:
Felix Ungar

Actor and musician who starred in over 60 films including Mister Roberts (1955), Some Like It Hot (1959), The Apartment (1960), The Great Race (1965), The Odd Couple and its sequel 30 years later, The Odd Couple II, Save the Tiger (1973), The China Syndrome (1979), Missing (1982) and Grumpy Old Men (1993). Lemmon was nominated eight times for an Academy Award, winning twice for his roles in Mister Roberts and Save The Tiger.

Walter Matthau
Born: 1st October 1920
Died: 1st July 2000

Character:
Oscar Madison

Actor and comedian best known for his role as Oscar Madison in The Odd Couple and his frequent collaborations with Odd Couple co-star Jack Lemmon, particularly in the 1990's with Grumpy Old Men and its sequel Grumpier Old Men. Matthau won the Academy Award for Best Supporting Actor for his performance in the Billy Wilder film The Fortune Cookie (1966). Besides the Oscar, he was also the winner of two BAFTA's, a Golden Globe and two Tony awards.

John Donald Fiedler
Born: 3rd February 1925
Died: 25th June 2005

Character:
Vinnie

Actor and voice actor who was slight, balding, and bespectacled, with a distinctive high-pitched voice. His career lasted more than 55 years on stage, film, television and radio. He is best known for four roles; the nervous Juror No.2 in 12 Angry Men, the voice of Piglet in Disney's Winnie The Pooh, Vinnie, one of Oscar's poker cronies in the film version of Neil Simon's The Odd Couple, and Mr. Peterson, the hen-pecked milquetoast on The Bob Newhart Show.

TRIVIA

Goofs | In the opening scenes, when Felix is walking into the go-go dancer club, a woman with long brown hair is leaving. When Felix enters the club she is dancing on stage.

During the first poker game Vinnie is dealt two Queens, a Ten, a Nine and a Four, in full view of the camera (and the other players). At the draw he asks for no cards but then proceeds to win the hand after announcing he has a Straight.

Interesting Facts | This is the second of ten films in which the two great friends, Jack Lemmon and Walter Matthau, are paired.

CONTINUED

Interesting Facts

Walter Matthau, who played Oscar in both the original Broadway play and the movie, asked the play's author, Neil Simon, if he could play Felix instead. This was because Matthau thought Oscar's personality was too similar to his own and the role would be too easy; whereas playing the persnickety Felix would be a real acting challenge. Simon replied, "Walter, go and be an actor in somebody else's play. Please be Oscar in mine." Matthau finally agreed to it.

According to former Paramount production chief Robert Evans in his memoir 'The Kid Stays In The Picture', producer Howard Koch originally wanted to use the Broadway cast, Walter Matthau (Oscar) and Art Carney (Felix) in the movie. Evans wanted Jack Lemmon for Felix and Billy Wilder, who directed Lemmon and Matthau in The Fortune Cookie (1966), as writer-director. The cost for the Lemmon-Matthau-Wilder package was $3 million plus 50% of the profits. Paramount owner Charlie Bluhdorn balked at the demands and personally took over negotiations. Wilder eventually dropped out. Lemmon was signed for $1 million against 10% of the gross and Matthau got a straight salary of $300,000.

The Odd Couple was reportedly Paramount's biggest hit since The Ten Commandments (1956).

Quotes

Oscar Madison: I can't take it anymore, Felix, I'm cracking up. Everything you do irritates me. And when you're not here, the things I know you're gonna do when you come in irritate me. You leave me little notes on my pillow. Told you 158 times I can't stand little notes on my pillow. 'We're all out of cornflakes. F.U.' Took me three hours to figure out F.U. was Felix Ungar!

(Felix is making weird noises in the diner)
Oscar Madison: Stop that, will ya? What are you doing?
Felix Ungar: I'm trying to clear up my ears! Fmuh! Fmuh! You create a pressure inside your head, HMAHHH! Opens up the Eustachian tubes. HMAHH! HMAAHH! HMAH-huh! FMAAAAAHHH!
(The other customers look at him strangely)
Oscar Madison: Did it open up?
Felix Ungar: Uh-huh, I think I sprained my throat. Eh-eh-eh-eh-eh-eh.

BULLITT

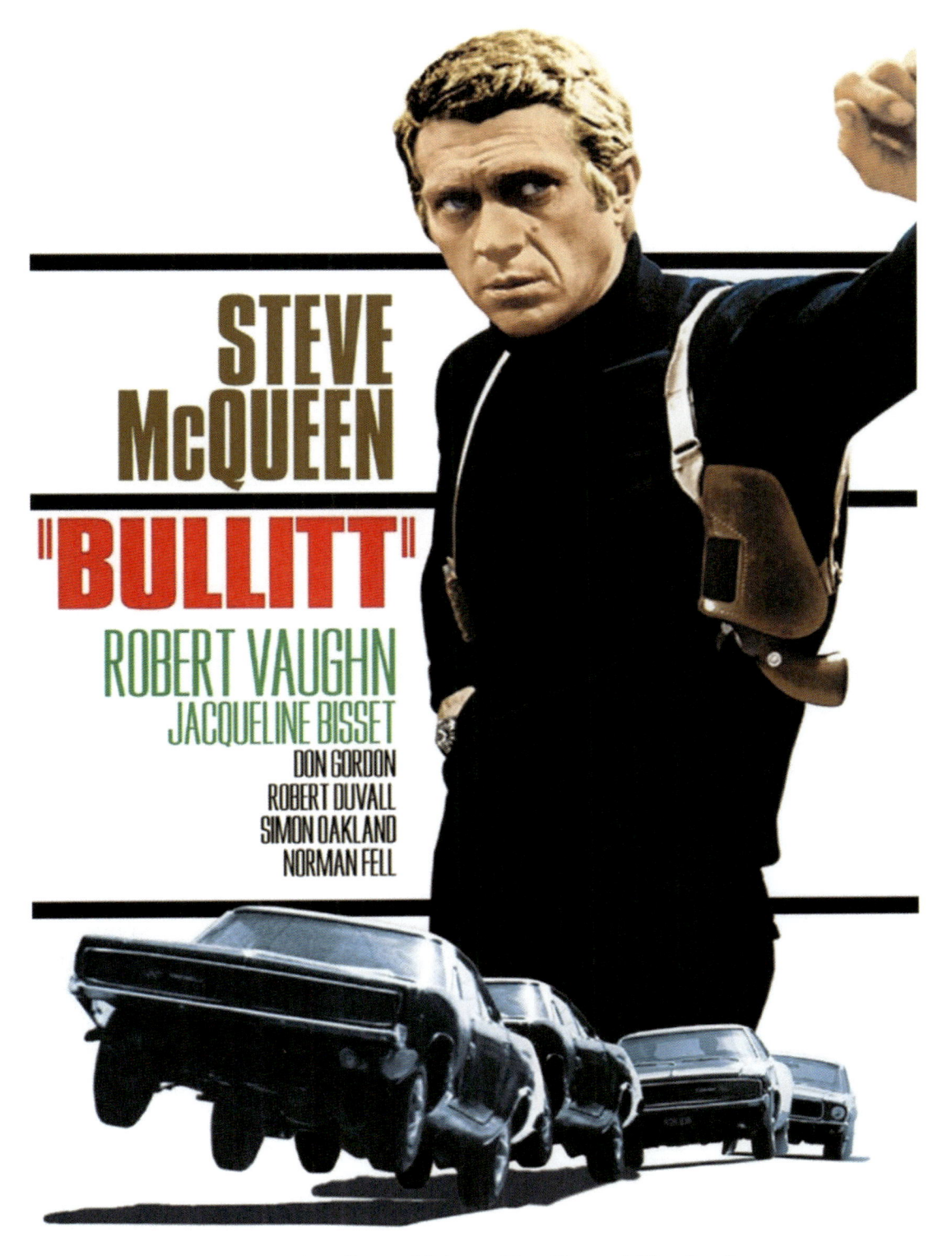

STEVE McQUEEN
"Bullitt"
ROBERT VAUGHN
JACQUELINE BISSET
DON GORDON
ROBERT DUVALL
SIMON OAKLAND
NORMAN FELL

Directed by: Peter Yates - Runtime: 114 minutes

An all guts no glory San Francisco cop becomes determined to find the underworld kingpin that killed the witness in his protection.

STARRING

Steve McQueen
Born: 24th March 1930
Died: 7th November 1980

Character:
Frank Bullitt

Actor often referred to as 'The King of Cool'. His most popular films include The Cincinnati Kid (1965), The Thomas Crown Affair (1968), Bullitt, The Getaway (1972), Papillon (1973), as well as the all-star ensemble films The Magnificent Seven (1960), The Great Escape (1963) and The Towering Inferno (1974). McQueen received an Academy Award nomination for his role in The Sand Pebbles (1966) and by 1974 he was the highest-paid movie star in the world.

Robert Vaughn
Born: 22nd November 1932
Died: 11th November 2016

Character:
Walter Chalmers

Actor noted for his stage, film and television work. His best-known TV roles include suave spy Napoleon Solo in The Man from U.N.C.L.E., General Hunt Stockwell in The A-Team and Albert Stroller in the British television drama series Hustle (2004-2012). Popular films include The Magnificent Seven (1960), Bullitt and Superman III (1983). For his role in The Young Philadelphians (1959) he was nominated for an Academy Award for Best Supporting Actor.

Jacqueline Bisset
Born: 13th September 1944

Character:
Cathy

Actress who first came to prominence in 1968 with roles in The Detective, Bullitt, and The Sweet Ride. In the 1970s she starred in Airport (1970), Day For Night (1973), Murder On The Orient Express (1974), The Deep (1977) and Who Is Killing The Great Chefs of Europe? (1978). In 2010 she received France's highest honour, the Légion d'honneur, with French President Nicolas Sarkozy calling her 'a movie icon'.

TRIVIA

Goofs | During the chase sequence the same green Volkswagen Beetle is seen at least 4 different times, in 4 different locations, in a period of not more than 1 minute.

The Dodge Charger which supposedly explodes at the gas station can still be seen in the background during the explosion.

Interesting Facts | Bullitt's reverse burnout during the chase scene actually wasn't in the script - Steve McQueen had mistakenly missed the turn but they decided to keep the footage.

CONTINUED

Interesting Facts | While filming the scene where the giant airliner taxis just above Steve McQueen, observers were shocked that no double was used. Asked if the producers couldn't have found a dummy, the actor wryly replied, "They did."

In 1968 San Francisco was not a big filmmaking mecca but the mayor, Joseph L. Alioto, was very keen to promote it as such. Consequently 'Bullitt' enjoyed a freedom of movement around the city that would be hard to come by today, including giving up an entire hospital wing for filming, closing down multiple streets for three weeks for a car chase scene and taking over San Francisco International Airport at night.

Robert Vaughn, who plays politician Walter Chalmers, received the script and didn't like it. He felt that there was no plot or a sensible story line. Steve McQueen insisted Vaughn do the film but the actor refused until the studio finally offered him so much money he finally said yes.

Quote | **Walter Chalmers:** Frank, we must all compromise.
Frank Bullitt: Bullshit.

Sporting Winners

BBC SPORTS PERSONALITY OF THE YEAR

David Hemery - Athletics

David Peter Hemery, CBE (b. 18th July 1944) is a former track and field athlete who won the 400 metres hurdles at the 1968 Summer Olympics in Mexico City.

1968	BBC Sports Personality Results	Country	Sport
Winner	**David Hemery**	**England**	**Athletics**
Runner Up	Graham Hill	England	Formula One
Third Place	Marion Coakes	England	Show Jumping

At the Mexico City Olympics Hemery won the 400m hurdles in 48.12 seconds, a new world record. His margin of victory was the largest since the 1924 Summer Olympics in Paris, beating second-placed Gerhard Hennige from West Germany by almost a second. Hemery's teammate John Sherwood came third to take the bronze medal.

Major Championship Medals:

Year	Competition	Location	Event	Medal
1966	Commonwealth Games	Kingston, Jamaica	120y Hurdles	Gold
1968	Olympic Games	Mexico City, Mexico	400m Hurdles	Gold
1969	European Championships	Athens, Greece	110m Hurdles	Silver
1970	Commonwealth Games	Edinburgh, Scotland	110m Hurdles	Gold
1972	Olympic Games	Munich, Germany	4x400m Relay	Silver
1972	Olympic Games	Munich, Germany	400m Hurdles	Bronze

After his running career Hemery worked as a coach in the United States and Great Britain. In 1998 he was elected as the first president of UK Athletics and in 2011 became the first Briton to be awarded the European Olympic Committee's Laurel Award for services to sport.

Five Nations Rugby
France

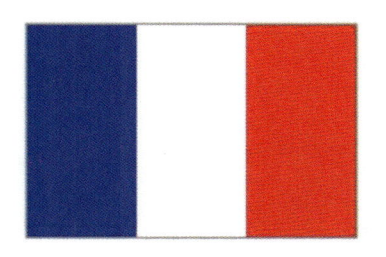

Position	Nation	Played	Won	Draw	Lost	For	Against	Points
1	**France**	**4**	**4**	**0**	**0**	**52**	**30**	**8**
2	Ireland	4	2	1	1	38	37	5
3	England	4	1	2	1	37	40	4
4	Wales	4	1	1	2	31	34	3
5	Scotland	4	0	0	4	18	35	0

The 1968 Five Nations Championship was the thirty-ninth series of the rugby union Five Nations Championship. Including the previous incarnations as the Home Nations and Five Nations, this was the seventy-fourth series of the northern hemisphere rugby union championship. Ten matches were played between the 13th January and 23rd March. It was contested by England, France, Ireland, Scotland and Wales, and marked the first Grand Slam victory for France.

Date	Team	Score	Team	Location
13/01/1968	Scotland	6-8	France	Edinburgh
20/01/1968	England	11-11	Wales	London
27/01/1968	France	16-6	Ireland	Paris
03/02/1968	Wales	5-0	Scotland	Cardiff
10/02/1968	England	9-9	Ireland	London
24/02/1968	France	14-9	England	Paris
24/02/1968	Ireland	14-6	Scotland	Dublin
09/03/1968	Ireland	9-6	Wales	Dublin
16/03/1968	Scotland	6-8	England	Edinburgh
23/03/1968	Wales	9-14	France	Cardiff

Teams	-	Venues	-	Team Captains
France	-	Stade Olympique	-	Christian Carrère
Ireland	-	Lansdowne Road	-	Tom Kiernan
England	-	Twickenham	-	Colin MacFadyean / Mike Weston
Wales	-	National Stadium	-	Norman Gale / Gareth Edwards / John Dawes
Scotland	-	Murrayfield	-	Pringle Fisher / Jim Telfer

Calcutta Cup

Scotland 6-8 England

The Calcutta Cup was first awarded in 1879 and is the rugby union trophy awarded to the winner of the match (currently played as part of the Six Nations Championship) between England and Scotland.

1968 British Grand Prix - Jo Siffert

Chris Amon (left) and Jacky Ickx flank Swiss driver Jo Siffert at the 1968 British Grand Prix.

The 1968 British Grand Prix was a Formula One motor race held at the Brands Hatch Circuit on the 20th July 1968. It was race 7 of 12 in both the 1968 World Championship of Drivers and the 1968 International Cup for Formula One Manufacturers. The race was held over 80 laps of the 2.65 mile circuit giving a total race distance of 212 miles. After starting from fourth place on the grid the race was won by Lotus-Ford driver Jo Siffert, his first Formula One victory and the first victory by a Swiss driver. Second and third places were taken by Ferrari drivers Chris Amon (NZ) and Jacky Ickx (BEL).

1968 Formula 1 - Season Summary

The 1968 Formula One season was the 22nd season of the FIA's Formula One motor racing and featured the 19th FIA World Championship. The first of the 12 races started on the 1st January 1968 in South Africa and ended on the 3rd November in Mexico. Graham Hill won the second of his two Formula One World Drivers Championships with race wins in Spain, Monaco and Mexico.

Pos.	Country	Driver	Constructor	Race Wins	Points
1	**United Kingdom**	**Graham Hill**	**Lotus-Ford**	**3**	**48**
2	United Kingdom	Jackie Stewart	Matra-Ford	3	36
3	New Zealand	Denny Hulme	McLaren-Ford	2	33
4	Belgium	Jacky Ickx	Ferrari	1	27
5	New Zealand	Bruce McLaren	McLaren-Ford	1	22

Jim Clark: The first race of the 1968 season was won by two time F1 World Champion Jim Clark (1963, 1965). Tragically he was killed just 3 months later on the 7th April in a motor racing accident at Hockenheim, Germany. At the time of his death he had won more Grand Prix races (25) and achieved more Grand Prix pole positions (33) than any other driver. In 2009 The Times placed Clark at the top of a list of the greatest-ever Formula One drivers.

Grand National
Red Alligator

The 1968 Grand National was the 122nd renewal of this world famous horse race and took place at Aintree Racecourse near Liverpool on the 30th March. Red Alligator, trained by Denys Smith and ridden by Brian Fletcher, won the race by 20 lengths. Brian Fletcher would later go on to ride Red Rum to his 1973 and 1974 Grand National victories.

	Name	Jockey	Age	Weight	Odds
1st	**Red Alligator**	**Brian Fletcher**	**9**	**10st**	**100/7**
2nd	Moidore's Token	Barry Brogan	11	10st 8lb	100/6
3rd	Different Class	David Mould	8	11st 5lb	17/2
4th	Rutherfords	Pat Buckley	8	10st 6lb	100/9
5th	The Fossa	Roy Edwards	11	10st 4lb	28/1

45 Runners: 17 Finished / 4 Pulled Up / 12 Fell / 5 Brought Down / 7 Refused

Epsom Derby
Sir Ivor

The Derby Stakes is Britain's richest horse race and the most prestigious of the country's five Classics. First run in 1780 this Group 1 flat horse race is open to three year old thoroughbred colts and fillies. It is run at Epsom Downs in Surrey over a distance of one mile, four furlongs and 10 yards (2,423 metres) and is scheduled for early June each year.

Photo: American-bred, Irish-trained, Thoroughbred racehorse and sire Sir Ivor (1965-1995), returns to the winners enclosure with jockey Lester Piggott after winning the 1968 Derby.

Football League Champions

England

Pos.	Team	F	A	Points
1	**Manchester City**	**86**	**43**	**58**
2	Manchester United	89	55	56
3	Liverpool	71	40	55
4	Leeds United	71	41	53
5	Everton	67	40	52

Scotland

Pos.	Team	F	A	Points
1	**Celtic**	**106**	**24**	**63**
2	Rangers	93	34	61
3	Hibernian	67	49	45
4	Dunfermline Athletic	64	41	39
5	Aberdeen	63	48	37

FA Cup Winners - West Bromwich Albion

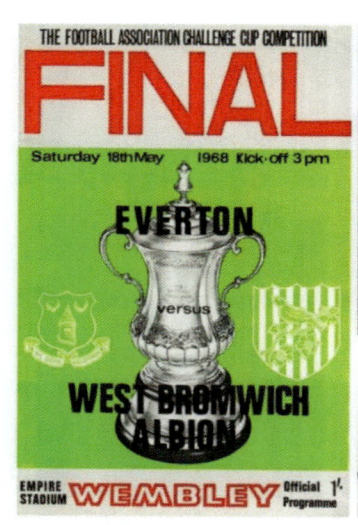

West Bromwich Albion   1-0   Everton
Jeff Astle ⚽ 93'

Referee: Leo Callaghan - Attendance: 100,000

The 1968 FA Cup Final took place on the 18th May at Wembley Stadium with West Brom winning by a single goal, scored by Jeff Astle three minutes into extra time. The goal meant that Astle had scored in every round of that season's competition. The Cup Final was the first to be televised live in colour and was West Brom's fifth Cup win.

GOLF - THE OPEN CHAMPIONSHIP
GARY PLAYER

The 1968 Open Championship was the 97th to be played and was held between the 10th and 13th July at Carnoustie Golf Links, Angus, Scotland. Gary Player won the second of his three Open titles, two strokes ahead of runners-up Bob Charles and Jack Nicklaus, to take the Claret Jug and winner's prize money of £3,000. It was the fifth of Player's nine major titles.

SNOOKER - JOHN PULMAN

With the agreement of the Billiards Association and Control Council the World Snooker Championship was revived by Rex Williams on a challenge basis after a six-year absence in 1964. The 1957 World Champion John Pulman remained unbeaten after playing seven challenge matches against various opponents from 1964-1969. The tournament then reverted back to a knock-out tournament in 1969.

Year	Winner	Score	Opponent	Venue
1964	John Pulman	19-16	Fred Davis	Burroughes Hall, London
1964	John Pulman	40-33	Rex Williams	Burroughes Hall, London
1965	John Pulman	37-36	Fred Davis	Burroughes Hall, London
1965	John Pulman	25-22	Rex Williams	South Africa
1965	John Pulman	39-12	Fred van Rensburg	South Africa
1966	John Pulman	5-2	Fred Davis	St George's Hall, Liverpool
1968	John Pulman	39-34	Eddie Charlton	Co-operative Hall, Bolton

WIMBLEDON

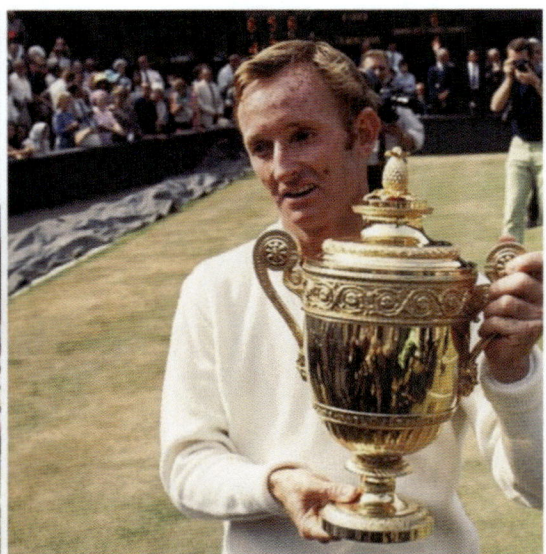

Mens Singles Champion - Rod Laver - Australia
Ladies Singles Champion - Billie Jean King - United States

The 1968 Wimbledon Championships took place on the outdoor grass courts at the All England Lawn Tennis and Croquet Club in Wimbledon, London, and ran from the 24th June until the 6th July. It was the 82nd staging of the Wimbledon Championships and the third Grand Slam tennis event of 1968.

Men's Singles Final:

Country	Player	Set 1	Set 2	Set 3
Australia	Rod Laver	6	6	6
Australia	Tony Roche	3	4	2

Women's Singles Final:

Country	Player	Set 1	Set 2
United States	Billie Jean King	7	9
Australia	Judy Tegart	5	7

Men's Doubles Final:

Country	Players	Set 1	Set 2	Set 3	Set 4	Set 5
Australia	John Newcombe / Tony Roche	3	8	5	14	6
Australia	Ken Rosewall / Fred Stolle	6	6	7	12	3

Women's Doubles Final:

Country	Players	Set 1	Set 2	Set 3
United States	Rosemary Casals / Billie Jean King	3	6	7
France / United Kingdom	Françoise Dürr / Ann Haydon-Jones	6	4	5

Mixed Doubles Final:

Country	Players	Set 1	Set 2
Australia	Ken Fletcher / Margaret Court	6	14
Soviet Union	Alex Metreveli / Olga Morozova,	1	12

1968 Summer Olympics

The 1968 Summer Olympics, officially known as the Games of the XIX Olympiad, were held in Mexico City, Mexico, in October 1968. These were the first Olympic Games to be staged in Latin America and the first to be staged in a Spanish-speaking country. The Games were also the first to use an all-weather (smooth) track for track and field events instead of the traditional cinder track.

British Gold Medallists:

Competitor	Discipline	Event
David Hemery	Athletics	4x100m Hurdles
Chris Finnegan	Boxing	Men's Middleweight
Derek Allhusen, Jane Bullen, Ben Jones, Richard Meade	Equestrian	Three-Day Event Team Competition
Bob Braithwaite	Shooting	Men's Trap Shooting
Rodney Pattisson, Iain MacDonald-Smith	Sailing	Men's Flying Dutchman

Medals Table - Top 5 Countries:

Rank	Nation	Gold	Silver	Bronze	Total
1	United States	45	28	34	107
2	Soviet Union	29	32	30	91
3	Japan	11	7	7	25
4	Hungary	10	10	12	32
5	East Germany	9	9	7	25
10	**Great Britain**	**5**	**5**	**3**	**13**

Controversy: During the medal ceremony for the men's 200m race American athletes Tommie Smith (gold) and John Carlos (bronze) made a Black Power salute by raising their black-gloved fists during the American national anthem. As punishment the IOC banned Smith and Carlos from the Olympic Games for life.

The Cost Of Living

**Wave After Wave.
Drink After Drink.**

You ride the big one
all the way in.
Then: Coca-Cola, splashing
over your thirst.
Cold. Fresh. With that
one-of-a-kind taste.
Coke has the taste
you never get tired of.
It makes the best things
in life go even better.
Like the perfect wave.
Like anything.

Things go better with Coke

Comparison Chart

	1968 Price	1968 Price (Including Inflation)	2017 Price	Real Term % Change
3 Bedroom House	£5,200	£86,806	£226,000	+160.3%
Weekly Income	£11.8s.2d	£190.45	£530	+178.3%
Pint Of Beer	1s.2d	97p	£3.47	+258.8%
Cheese (lb)	4s.8d	£3.90	£3.25	-16.7%
Bacon (lb)	6s.6d	£5.43	£3.63	-33.1%
The Beano	4d	28p	£2.50	+792.9%

SHOPPING

Kangaroo Butter (½lb pack)	1s.5d
Jacobs Cream Crackers	10d
Sainsbury's English Cheddar Cheese (lb)	3s.2d
Dutch Edam Cheese (lb)	3s.4d
Branston Pickle (family jar)	2s.8d
Heinz Vegetable Soup (10½oz)	10d
Sainsbury's Tomato Soup (1lb 12oz family size)	1s.6d
Crosse & Blackwell Baked Beans (16oz)	11½d
New Potatoes (1lb 3oz can)	1s.9d
Marela Pickled Onions (30oz)	3s.6d
Paxo Stuffing	8d
Princes Prawns (7½oz)	3s.4d
Fruit Cocktail (15½oz)	1s.11d
Peach Slices (large)	2s.3d
Fine Fare Creamed Rice (15½oz)	10d
Strawberries In Syrup (15oz)	2s
Mrs Peeks Christmas Pudding (2lb)	4s.4d
Seedless Satsumas (x7)	2s
Nescafe	4s.6d
Maxwell House Instant Coffee (4oz)	4s
Ty-Phoo Tea (¼lb)	1s.4½d
Sainbury's Red Label Tea (¼lb)	1s.3d
Nestlés Cream (6oz)	1s
Schweppes Mineral Water	10d
Sainsbury's Cola (can)	8½d
Whole Orange Drink	1s.10d
Crawford's Tartan Shortbread Biscuits (7½oz)	1s.7d
Smiths Crisps (family pack)	1s.8d
Robertson's Mincemeat (14¼oz)	1s.8d
Cadbury's Milk Tray	6s.11d
After Eight Mints	3s.9d
Victory V Lozenges (pack)	10d
365 Family Shampoo	3s.2d
365 Hairspray	3s.9d
Dixcel Toilet Rolls (twin pack)	1s.4d
Boots Baby Lotion	2s.3d
Savlon Antiseptic Cream (small)	2s.6d
Ultra Brite Toothpaste (standard size tube)	3s.8d
Omo Washing Powder (family size)	2s.9d
Fynnon Spa Bath Salts	2s.6d

A Fresh Brillo Pad Saves Time

Give your chips yum, mum.

And your fish.
And shepherd's pie. And sausages.
Not to mention cold meat salad.
And stew. The lot, in fact.
 The fabulous HP Sauce adds taste to it all. Good, rich, spicy taste that makes food a little bit special.
 For dad. And the children.
And you, dear mum.
 The fabulous HP Sauce.

We're really sockin' it to you this Christmas

With the Hottest Hits ever.

1. "THE BEATLES" double album	73/-
2. THE ROLLING STONES—Beggars' Banquet	36/8
3. JIMI HENDRIX EXPERIENCE—Electric Ladyland double album	72/2
4. JETHRO TULL—This Was	37/8
5. CANNED HEAT—Livin' the Blues double album	62/9
6. THE PENTANGLE—Sweet Child double album	69/6
7. BIG BROTHER & THE HOLDING CO. (featuring MISS JANIS IAN)—Cheap Thrills	36/8
8. THE KINKS VILLAGE GREEN PRESERVATION SOCIETY	36/6

FROM ALL SHOPS WITH RECORD DEPARTMENTS

W. H. SMITH & SON

CLOTHES

Women's Clothing

Swears & Wells Musquash Fur Coat	98gns
Marshall Ward Party Dress	£2.14s
Orlon Arran Pattern Cardigan	£2.12s.6d
Evans Long Sleeved Jumper	£1.15s
Hard Wearing Cord Pinafore	£1.9s.11d
Casual Cotton Sweater (x2)	£1.8s
Ladies Stretch Slacks	£2.5s
Tweed Skirt	£1.1s
Crimplene ¾ Lined Skirt	£1.7s.6d
Mod Mini Kilt	£2.7s
Marshall Ward Ladies High Boots	£2.17s.6d

Men's Clothing

Burtons Wool & Angora Overcoat	£12.10s
Terylene & Wool Made To Measure Suit	£10.19s.6d
Harris Tweed Jacket	£7.19s.6d
Marshall Ward Acrylic Pullover	£1.9s.11d
Knitted Cotton Sweater (x2)	£1.19s
John Collier Trousers	£2.9s.6d
Leather Look Chelsea Boots	£1.7s.6d

SAY, SISTERS, WHAT IS THIS FREEDOM?

To run in the wind, little sister,
To wear only your own second nature.
That is the freedom of Berlei
…the new name of liberty.
In pink, bra 8007 **27/11**
…girdle 7183 **39/11**
In black, bra 506 **32/6**
(D cup **37/6**)
…girdle 772 **44/-**
In white, bra 401X. **19/11**
…girdle 792 **49/11**
Nearly all in other colours.

Win the beautiful world of *Berlei*

LEVI'S WESTERN WEAR

501 LEVI'S Blue denim jeans, button. Also style 502 with zip fly.

557 LEVI'S blue denim jacket.

RUGGED!

The Old West worked hard – and lived hard. Horses, Indians, Rustlers, Law. Today it moves peacefully on wings, wheels, rotor blades. Only LEVI'S jeans have stood the changing strains of Western life since 1850 – all over the world.

Levi's

the **original** blue jeans world famous since 1850.

208 listen to Levi's on Radio Luxembourg Top 20 every Sunday Night

See the whole LEVI'S range in the lavish, all-colour 1968 brochure. This coupon brings your copy.

7304 LEVI'S blue denim western shirt.

Sole U.K. LEVI'S Distributors: F.J. Gertler & Co. Ltd., **Dept. W16** Avon Trading Estate, Block L, Avonmore Road, London, W.14.

NAME _____

ADDRESS _____

ALWAYS ASK FOR GENUINE LEVI'S BY NAME
LEVI'S FROM STOCKISTS **ONLY**— EVERYWHERE

TOYS

Raleigh Gresham Flyer Junior Bicycle	£15.14s.4d
Tri-Ang Junior Pedal Car	£3.15s.6d
Dumpy Sit 'n' Ride Excavator Tractor	£3.9s.6d
Trampoline	£4.19s.6d
Crybaby Tearie Dearie Doll	£1.2s.6d
Speed King Electric Motor Racing Set	£2.19s.6d
Jacko Monkey	£2.2s.6d
Marshall Ward Battery Operated Train Set	£1.9s.6d
Blackboard & Easel	£1.1s
Table Tennis Set	12s
Compendium Of 6 Games	9s.6d
Lone Star Cowboy Holster Set	12s
Pretty Tammy Doll	7s.6d
Modern Miss Pastry Set	6s.6d
Siren Police Car	£1.9s.6d

POW — DIRECT FROM GOTHAM CITY

GIFT SET No. 3
Batman's Batmobile and Batboat.
Overall length 10¼ inches 267 mm.

Available separately:
107 Batboat on Trailer
5½ inches 140 mm.

Available separately:
267 Batmobile
5 inches 127 mm.

Plus a Batman Badge to fix on your coat lapel or shirt.

BATMAN

266 Chitty Chitty Bang Bang
6½ inches 162 mm.
Albert R. Broccoli presents Ian Fleming's Chitty Chitty Bang Bang — A Warfield Production.
© 1967 Glidrose Productions Ltd. & Warfield Productions Ltd.

Chitty Chitty Bang Bang

803 The Beatles' Yellow Submarine
5¼ inches 133 mm.
© 1968 King Features Syndicate & Subafilms Ltd.

MONKEEMOBILE
277 The Monkees' Monkeemobile
4¾ inches 123 mm.
Trade Mark of Screen Gems Inc.
© 1968 Raybert Productions Inc.

JAMES BOND
270 James Bond Aston Martin DB5
4 inches 102 mm.
© 1967 Glidrose Productions Ltd. & Eon Productions Ltd.

61

LOOK SHARP!
and hear the difference

SHARP Model RD504 Portable Tape Recorder

An all-transistor solid state Tape Recorder. For operation by batteries or AC mains, twin track, two speeds. Superb recording and reproduction. Plug in to the mains. It automatically changes from batteries to its built-in AC power unit. Remote control switch on microphone allows full flexibility in use. Dimensions: 12"x3¾"x9¼" Complete with dynamic microphone, recording lead, earphone, batteries (6x sharp UM—1) 5" tape reel, empty spool.

Hearing's believing. Come and talk yourself into a SHARP vivid sound tape recorder.

SHARP

Sharp SALES & SERVICE,
16/18 WORSLEY ROAD, SWINTON, MANCHESTER. Tel: SWI 3232 (5 lines)

26 GNS

for further details & colour leaflet contact
SHARP SALES & SERVICE
16/18 WORSLEY RD., SWINTON, MANCHESTER

NAME..
ADDRESS..
....
....

ELECTRICAL ITEMS

19in Bush Television Set (b/w)	68gns
Kenwood Mixer	£34.17s.6d
Morphy Richards Steam & Spray Iron	£6.16s.11d
Prinz Stereo Hi-Fi Record Player	47gns
Westminster Record Player	12gns
Dixons Portable Cassette Tape Recorder	£22.19s.6d
Electrolux Electric Radiator	£15.16s.1d
Concorde Double Electric Blanket	£4.12s.6d
Kenwood Heated Rollers (set of 18)	£12.19s.6d
Philips Twin Turbo 'T' Fan	£8.3s.1d
Remmington Selectric Shaver	£9.9s
Black & Decker GD25 ½in Power Drill	£14.19s.6d
Black & Decker HD1215 9in Circular Power Saw	£29.10s

EXCITEMENT!!!

4-stroke engine with **Overhead Camshaft** and chain drive.

The New Honda 50 Super Cub has everything! Automatic clutch, one-piece leg shields, dual seat, fully sprung pressed steel frame, flashing trafficators, mirrors, speedometer. And all this for £104-19-0 (incl. all taxes).

HONDA
WORLD'S LARGEST MOTORCYCLE MANUFACTURERS

Other Prices

Morris Oxford De Luxe	£904
Hillman Minx Standard Saloon	£828
Lexden 3-Piece Suite	£72.9s.6d
Silentnight Silver Ribbon Super De-Luxe 4ft 6in Divan Set	£39.19s.6d
Teak Style Fireplace Surround	£7.12s.6d
Rotary Clothes Dryer	£2.19s.6d
Tower 5-Tread Platform Steps	£1.9s.11d
MFI Luxury Carpet (per yard, 18in wide)	4s.9d
Kent 6ft x 4ft Shed	£18.10s
Topdec Gloss White Paint (pint)	6s.9d
Jones Sewing Machine	28gns
Kodak Instamatic Camera	£7.2s.6d
Ladies 9ct Gold, Golden Treasure Rotary Watch	£2.1s
Haig Whisky	£2.9s.11d
Seagers Cream Australian Sherry	12s.11d
Don Cortez Spanish Wine (large bottle)	11s.9d
Player's No.10 Cigarettes (20)	3s.3d
Senior Service Cigarettes (20)	3s.6d
Minatella Cigars (20)	7s.2d
Womans Realm Magazine	7d
TV Times	9d
Radio Times	8d

Don't change the grade, change the brand.

If your car needs the best petrol, you won't save anything by switching to a lower grade. It could cost you more in the long run.
What you should do is to switch companies.
Because Esso's two top-grade petrols, Esso Extra and Esso Plus, are cheaper than the same grades offered by our four nearest competitors.
Remember, Esso petrols have always been good value and top quality. Now you can save money despite this extra 5d.
Don't change the grade, change the brand. Use Esso.

Esso Extra 6/4 Esso Plus 6/2 Esso 5/11

(Recommended retail prices for London and most large Cities).

The Lazy Fireball.

Vauxhall's new 3.3 litre Ventora.

Ventora is Vauxhall's new concept in motoring. New in feel, new in performance, new in safety. Because sleek, plushy Ventora, with its compact streamlined body and individual-style seating, is powered by a smooth 6-cylinder 140-horse fireball: extra power for effortless, long-striding luxury on the open road – plus lazy top-gear flexibility for town-traffic driving. That's Vauxhall's new Ventora. The lazy fireball.
Vivid acceleration, superb top-gear flexibility.
Sensational roadholding and handling.
Unique passenger safety engineering.
Power brakes. Front discs. Rear drums.
Optional Powerglide Automatic. Or Overdrive.
Optional black roof in grained Vinyl.
Great good looks from every angle; ultra-luxury interior.
And from only £1102 inc.pt.

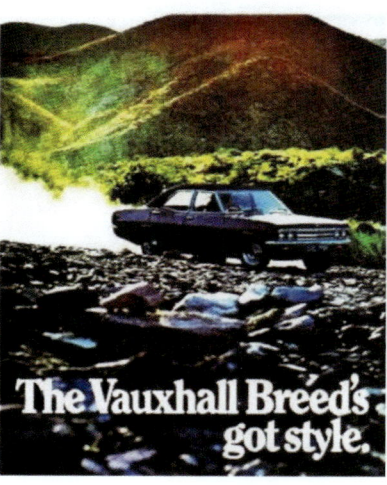

The Vauxhall Breed's got style.

Pre-Decimal Currency

Old Money		Equivalent Today
Farthing	¼d	0.1p
Half Penny	½d	0.21p
Penny	1d	0.42p
Threepence	3d	1.25p
Sixpence	6d	2.5p
Shilling	1s	5p
Florin	2s	10p
Half Crown	2s.6d	12.5p
Crown	5s	25p
Ten Shillings	10s	50p
Pound	20s	£1
Guinea	21s	£1.05

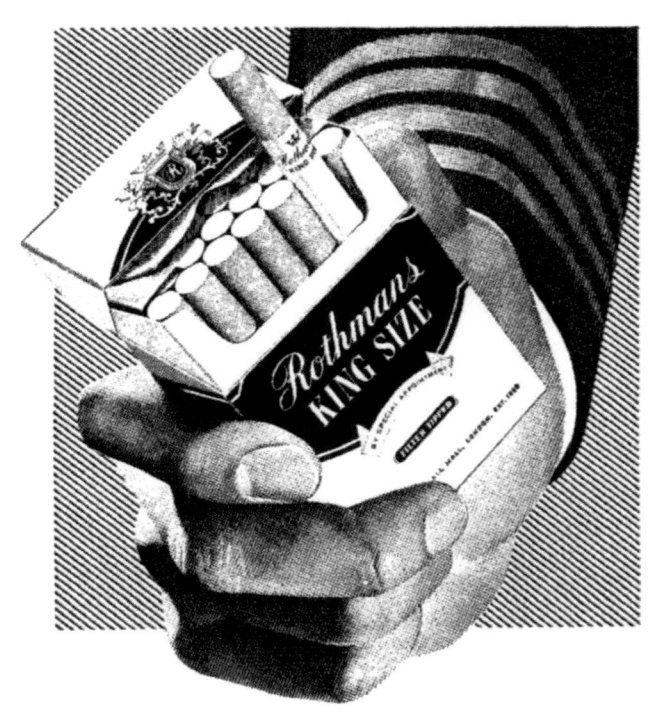

King Size Satisfaction

All over the world, in over 160 countries, on over 100 airlines the swing is to Rothmans King Size, Britain's most exported cigarette. There must be a reason why. It's simply this. Rothmans extra length, finer filter and the best tobacco money can buy give you true King Size flavour.

Rothmans-king size flavour that really satisfies

LAUGHTER

'There's only one snag—I can't read'

Printed in Great Britain
by Amazon